I Walked to the Moon
and Almost Everybody Waved

Have A Great Life

Your Friend
Ed Carlson
The Waver

'The Waver' returns to spread joy on local streets

By Scott Thomsen
GAZETTE-JOURNAL

JUN 06 1994   116 244

Reno is a friendlier city today following the return of Ed "Waver" Carlson.

About 30 people g... the Unity Ministr... Church Sunday to v... their wandering f... self-imposed, tw... cal in Iowa and li... his travels. Car... the waver for h... and smiling Th... walked U.S ... and Carson ...

"I love ... with sm... waves t... glad to ...

Aft... adm... wa...

South Virginia Street and the Mt. Rose Highway to the northwest Reno church wore him out. "I got tired," he said. "My feet are sore today."

Carlson, who has called Reno ... since 1974, has walked ...000 miles along the ...ways of Ameri-... His efforts ... "Rip-...

The Walker-and-waver

Having attracted a ... greater attendance with his first weekend spiritual get together than most Reno-... area public agencies can ... of South Virginia Street has ... scheduled another.

Ed Carlson, known ... Thousands of motorists ... his two years of ped... Reno, said abou... attended his ... meeting a h... This Is It ... Carls...

a more than 20,000 m... les in his journey. But 'recent' the time ha... settle do... hold r...

CED ... 1976

LIVING ON A WAVE

Reno institution Ed Carlson has walked 150,000 miles in 15 years

By Michael Sion/Gazette-Journal

DEC 21 1988   116-244

He walks and waves.
Drivers wave and honk.
A simple life. A simple message.
A man of weird extremes.
Like the smoot... stones he gathers from Lake Tahoe and gives out as "health stones," "strength stones," or "wisdom stones,"

Says Carlson "For 14 ye... walked from Carson to Reno in a straight line. Now I walk in circles around Reno."

"I missed you," says the man. "This is for you," says Carlson, and hands him one of his hand-written love messages, explaining ...alks and waves.

... freedom from the

Like the "love messages," handwritten in blue ball point, he hands to puzzled strangers, which read: "Years Ago, I Was Awakened To My Spirit, And I Found This Part Of Us Is All Loving, All Peaceful, All Understanding, And The Reason I Walk And Wave Is To Share The Love I Feel".

Like the periodic hitchhikes to New York, Los Angeles, San Francisco, traversing America 40-50 times.

Like the inaudible "kai-eeb" or "karcerum" he chants with each breath. "The effect of it is it calms my whole molecular structure. Even when I'm drinking beer, having sex, I'm meditating."

Like his notion the world is growing more peaceful — crises report ... in the media being in the minority of ... nts — and that the year 2003 will be that of heaven on earth.

1,000 Walks Later, Motorists Wave Back

'The Waver' walks to the beat of a different drummer

You know "The Waver?" The fellow with the graying reddish hair, who walks along the side of Hwy. 89A and Hwy. 179 and waves to everyone who passes by in a vehicle?

In these days of a predatory mentality of one-upmanship among the general populace, here is a man who genuinely dares to walk to the tune of a different drummer. I don't know his ~~name~~ guess I don't really nee~~d~~

I lived in Ren~~o~~ Waver wa~~s~~ has ~~b~~

~~l~~
~~n~~
~~he~~r
~~bac~~
Carso~~n~~
lunch
Mos~~t~~
more th~~an~~

By Michael Sion

t seems far-fe~~tched~~
downright flak~~y~~
scale war in the~~
But the way F~~
— the planet is g~~
peaceful by the day, g~~
notwithstanding.
And that's the word fr~~om~~
Waver.
Known by that moniker~~
full-time occupation of trea~~
Reno's sidewalks and road s,~~
since 1974, waving at passing~~
Carlson adheres to his predict~~ion
that the world will reach an ag~~
everlasting peace by the year 2~~

"Each day there's less hostility
This world is truly coming to a
goodness state," says Carlson on a
recent pre-war Friday in his self-
described "office" — a bench under
the big clock in Park Lane Mall.
"I truly couldn't be doing what
I've been doing for 18 years if I
didn't know that."

tures. But he keeps on doing what he does. I doubt that he is a rich man in financial terms. He probably doesn't even have a profit motive.

Here is a m~~an~~
a few who re~~
will in the liv~~
and unselfish~~

There was~~
~~t~~ of Waver~~s
~~w~~o went ou~~
waved a~~t
~~pa~~ssersby~~
~~if~~ you we~~
~~2~~ or c~~
~~l~~y m~~
~~or s~~
~~he~~

~~t~~

CATCHING THE WAVER

Reno's strolling philosopher still sees peace on horizon

Carlson's interaction with troubled young people.
"Around Christmas time, I've seen him in the mall, sitting there, talking to kids." Furchner says. "He just seems like a counselor. Talking to them, listening to them. Being like a big brother."
Reno optometrist Eric Kroll has provided Carlson with free eye care, including Lear Jet glasses.
"Ed sees the forest, he sees the universe, he sees the eternity of life," Kroll says. "That's why I love him. The Waver belongs to no church, subscribes to no religious dogma, although his very appearance suggests a spiritual dimension. He favors bright sweaters and New Ageish jewelry. He hands out smooth black stones from Lake Tahoe as tokens of health, wisdom and prosperity.
He says many assume his eccentricity translates into asceticism. In fact, he bar hops weekend nights.
"People put me in a category of

not doing human things," Carlson says. "When people see me drink, they see me doing human things, then they can relate to me."
He also is hardly anti-mater~~ial~~
The Waver could be seen last~~
a television advertisement f~~or
dealer Dick Donnelly.
"A few people said 'Yo~~
Ed,'" Carlson says with~~
But he says he has ne~~
money, and accepts wh~~
offer ($50 for the car~~
according to ad agen~~
Rogers).
"Nevada is the ~~
doesn't have a g~~
why I'm in New~~
Actually, Carl~~
guided to Reno~~
of 18 years w~~
taking their l~~
emotional re~~
By his ac~~
hardly one ~~
understan~~
Ramsey~~
drownin~~

The Wave:
'Bless you, brother'

JAN 1 9 1975

I WALKED TO THE MOON

AND ALMOST

EVERYBODY WAVED

REMARKABLE STORIES FROM
"THE WAVER'S"
22-YEAR JOURNEY FOR
LOVE AND PEACE

ED CARLSON
AS TOLD TO CLAIRE GERUS

✳ STILLPOINT PUBLISHING

✳STILLPOINT PUBLISHING

*Building a society that honors the Earth,
Humanity, and the Sacred in All Life*

For a free catalog or ordering information, write
Stillpoint Publishing, P.O. Box 640, Walpole, NH 03608
or call
1-800-847-4014 Toll Free (Continental US, except NH)
1-603-756-9281 (Foreign and NH)

This book was manufactured in the
United States of America.
Cover Design by Kathryn Sky-Peck
Text Design by Heather Gendron
Cover Photo Credits:
Author photograph: The Denver Post
Scenic photograph: Bonnie Sue

Published by Stillpoint Publishing, P.O. Box 640,
Meetinghouse Road, Walpole, NH 03608

ISBN: 1-883478-17-0
Library of Congress Catalog
Card Number: 96-069116

Dedication

To My Dear, Sweet Theresia

Table of Contents

PART III   HEALING THE SPIRIT

EPILOGUE

Acknowledgments

To all my dear friends I've met over the years and to the ones I haven't met yet.

I love you.

Thank you from the bottom of my heart.

— Ed Carlson
The Waver

Foreword

by Alan Cohen

When I first heard "The Waver's" story, I cried. Every time I hear "The Waver's" story, I cry. Not tears of sadness, but of sheer joy. If one man's life could be a long love letter, this is it.

I was driving through South Carolina when I popped Ed Carlson's tape, "I Walked to the Moon and Almost Everybody Waved," into the cassette player of my rental car. Before I even heard his story, my soul was soothed by Ed's voice; it was deep and resonant, and spoke from a heart connected to a most powerful source. I imagine Ed could have recited the alphabet, and I would have felt healed.

Then his story blew me away. "It came to me to hitchhike across the country blindfolded, to show that we could trust other people if we had no fear."

Excuse me? That was just the beginning. The saga that ensued grabbed me at a gut level, and I was riveted. My experience of Ed and his story was so compelling that I left my hotel room in the evenings and went down to the rental car to listen to the cassette. I needed to feel Ed's faith and absorb his practice of finding the good and the God in all people and experiences. I needed to be reminded that simplicity is more real than complexity. I needed to be taught that it is possible to live a Christ-like life even in these times.

Every now and then on his tape, Ed would stop his narrative and say to the listener, "I love you." And he would mean it. I would rewind to those points and feel nurtured in his caring. He meant it and I received it. What could be more important?

What Ed Carlson has done with his life is absolutely astounding. I see him as a model of faith and love in action. Many of us talk about a life founded in trust, but do we really practice it? Ed literally walks his talk. Now this remarkable man and his inspiring story are here for you to discover through the printed word. Perhaps "soak in" would be a better depiction. This is not a text for intellectual perusal; it is an adventure of the heart.

Every spiritual tradition advises us to seek the company of those who are dedicated to living the life of light. Here is a man with whom any human being would be blessed to share time and space. Ed's sparkling spirit is infused into these pages. Bask in them and you will find new life and renewed faith in your fellow human beings and yourself.

I don't know if I can put into words how much I love this man, and how much I respect how he lives. Ed Carlson has distilled the adventure of life to a simple principle: Give love. All other philosophies pale in the face of this noble truth, put into action. If your heart is hurting, read this book. If you need inspiration to find safety and beauty wherever you walk, read this book. If you want to learn how to love yourself, read this book.

If Christ returned today, I imagine he would be living much the way Ed Carlson is living. For years Ed has been waving to millions of people along America's highways. Now he waves to you through these pages. You're on the right road.

Remember Always the Truth.....
That You Are
Loved.....Special.....
and Important!

—Alan Cohen
author, *Joy is My Compass,* and
The Dragon Doesn't Live Here Anymore

Who Is "The Waver"?

by Claire Gerus

When I was first told about "The Waver," I had the same response most people probably do when they first encounter Ed Carlson: here's a well-meaning eccentric who spends his time walking around the country waving to people. God Bless Him.

But when I listened to Ed's tape describing his experiences, I realized that this man was more than a colorful character: he was following an inner sense of guidance to bring him to those people who needed to "experience" him. And that's the operative word, for anyone who meets Ed realizes very quickly that this is no ordinary man. This is an experience that will most likely change their lives.

The stories Ed tells are deceptively simple: a meeting with a derelict behind the Washington Monument brings both men important lessons in humility. A suicidal woman is saved by Ed's ability to show her how much there is to live for. A judge in the Midwest recognizes that love can find its rightful place in the courtroom.

Don't look for deep psychological insights here. The beauty of Ed's stories is in their simplicity. For Ed Carlson is a simple, yet dedicated man who, for 22 years, has followed a powerful inner calling to share love and peace with everyone he meets. His journey has taken him over 220,000 miles of arduous—sometimes dangerous—ground during his trek across the face of America. That's almost the equivalent of walking to the moon!

This book will be unlike any other book you've read, for Ed Carlson defies comparison, as does his life. He has made a calling of greeting his fellow man—and woman—with love. Sometimes he must to overcome derision, hostility and even violence. To everyone, he offers unconditional love. And everyone he meets is changed by the experience.

Ed is one of the most accepting people I've ever met. His nature is to give, totally. Often people give him money. Within an hour, Ed may have passed it on to someone in greater need. If his path takes him somewhere other than to his original destination, he welcomes the change, eagerly awaiting the gifts he can bring others he may now meet.

When Ed and I sat down to write about his experiences, I found myself overcome by the sheer magnitude of the people and events he's encountered as "The Waver." But as we explored these stories, I realized that each one stood on its own as a testimonial to one person's sheer determination to give love, no matter what. Ultimately, no one can remain unaffected when touched by the hand of love. We offer this book to everyone who may have questioned whether such goodness could exist in today's world.

Rest assured, love is alive and well. In fact, it's waiting for each one of us as we travel along our own personal highways. And if we're lucky, we'll meet someone like Ed Carlson along the way.

—Claire Gerus, Editor-in-Chief
Stillpoint Publishing
Walpole, New Hampshire
August, 1996

Why I Walk and Wave

My Dearest Ones:

I am asked why I walk and wave all the time.

Twenty-two years ago, I had a spiritual awakening, and it came to me that I should start walking to share the love I feel, and that I would be guided as to what to do.

Then, two years later while fasting at Lake Mead, Nevada, I had a vision, and I was told we are coming to an age of Peace on Earth and to gather everyone together as One.

So, my friends, I walk and wave, to help accomplish this through sharing pure, unconditional love.

All is Well. All is Love.

I love you.

—Ed Carlson,
The Waver

PART 1

Answering The Call

1

First Steps

Be still and know that all is love.

BEGINNINGS

I was born on March 7, 1937. I was a pretty cheerful kid with bright red hair. When I was still a young boy, my Mom would tell me, "Red, I don't know how you're going to do it, but one day you're going to make a lot of people happy."

I grew up, left home, and got married. Bonnie and I had four beautiful daughters, and I loved my family. But I was far from being a good husband. I just couldn't be stable. I was always going off on some new adventure, chasing rainbows with pots of sand at the end of them.

I never wanted to hurt anyone, especially those I loved the most. But something inside me just needed to break free, and even my family couldn't keep me reined in.

Finally, Bonnie left me. It broke my heart to lose her, but now I realize that this loss marked the end of one way of life, and the beginning of a new one. It was the first step on my journey to learn how to really love, and how to share that love with others.

BONNIE

It was just before my senior year in high school, and a guy I knew came up to me and said, "Hey, did you see that new blonde who moved into town?"

I had dated a good share of the local girls, but when he told me about Bonnie, I said to myself, "This is one I'm *not* going to date." But once I met her, I knew she was something special. And naturally, she was the girl I ended up marrying.

We got hitched after my basic training when I was on a three-day pass at Fort Knox, Kentucky. I got out of the Army in 1958 and worked in a box factory for two weeks. But I got bored with the work, and one day I threw the boxes up in the air, left Bonnie, and drove to Chicago.

She was devastated. As for me, I didn't know whether I'd be back or not. (I loved Bonnie so much and I do to this day, but now I know I was never meant to be a husband. I was meant to be a Waver. But it took me until I was 36 years old to find that out).

One day about a month later, I was talking to Bonnie over the phone. She was crying because it was our third anniversary, and I had forgotten it. When I hung up the phone, I felt so bad, I drove to Iowa and brought her back to Chicago with me.

Things settled down for awhile after that. Bonnie got a job at a law firm in the Chicago Loop, while I worked on the docks every night unloading trucks full of groceries. Together, we saved $1000 for me to go back to college.

In 1959, Bonnie and I left Chicago, and I enrolled at the University of Iowa. I went for half a semester, but one night, I got drunk, got in my car, and left for California.

Why did I do these things? At the time I didn't know it, but a plan was unfolding for me, and every step was bringing me closer to finding my path. I only wish it hadn't been so hard on the people who loved me.

FALLING

On my way to California, my car broke down in the Black Hills of South Dakota. I found a bar and went in to have a beer. A man walked in and asked if there were any log skidders in the room.

I said, "I am." I actually didn't know what a log skidder was, but I was curious to find out, and I needed some money. So I told him, "I'm strong and a good worker and I learn fast." All of which was true.

I ended up staying in the Black Hills for several months. Bonnie was still back in Chicago. Then, the night before our fourth anniversary, I got drunk and did some things that society would disapprove of for a married man. Then I began feeling guilty about Bonnie, who was always so faithful and loving.

So I got my old Plymouth going as fast as it would go and I crashed into a guard rail made out of telephone poles. The guard rail shattered and the car was demolished.

That was probably one of the lowest points in my life.

I remember sitting there in that wrecked car crying, "God, if you're there, I promise I'll devote my life to sharing it with others."

Then, a voice inside me said, "It's not time for you to do that yet. There's more for you to learn."

Those words proved to be so true. The days and years ahead would bring me a lot more pain and tears and confusion before I came out the other side. So I lived, and learned, and waited.

HITTING BOTTOM

Bonnie and I had been together on and off for fifteen years when she finally divorced me. A year later, she asked me to come back because of our daughters: Theresia, Sheley, Kristina and Cecelia.

So we stayed together for two more years. Then, on our 18th anniversary of being together, we were in Boston. We had all gone out for a picnic, and we had really had a great time. I thought, "Well, everything is going to come together now." Finally, after all those years, I felt ready to settle down.

But I guess it just wasn't meant to be. The next evening, I came home to find the apartment empty. I couldn't believe my eyes. Then, I knew. Bonnie had left me.

I ran to the door to throw myself in front of a streetcar. I didn't think I could go through life without my wife and my four wonderful daughters.

When I put my hand on the doorknob, and was about to turn it, I felt as if someone had hit me in the chest and knocked me to the floor. I screamed "God!" Then, I lay there for hours, crying and screaming. Finally, I begged, "If there's a God of any kind, please help me. I can't go on anymore in this confusion."

But there was no reply.

THE BREEZE

It took me a whole day to pull myself together. The next day, I decided to get out of the house and take a walk. Along the way, I saw some guys playing football, and figured that if I played some football and knocked some heads together, I'd get my mind off my own problems.

The guys said, "Sure, you can play." So I got down and started to throw a block into one of them, but something stopped me from hurting him. I just couldn't. So I stood up, and when I did, I felt a strange breeze sweep through me. It brought me a calm that I had never felt before. I didn't know it then, but that was The Beginning.

2

Walking in Blindness

We truly have no limitations.

BLINDFOLDED

I walked away from that football field, wondering what was going on. Something strange was happening, I knew that. Suddenly, my mind went back to a time five years earlier when I was doing summer theatre in Helena, Montana. I'd been studying my lines for a play about being blind, and I was really getting into my role. Suddenly, I had the thought that I should hitchhike across the United States—blindfolded—to understand how a blind person felt.

I didn't do it, of course. I just laughed the idea off and went back to memorizing my lines. But now I wondered why this thought should come back to me at this point in my life.

The idea kept nagging at me, so one week after the incident with the football players, I went to a drugstore. There, I bought two black patches with elastic on them.

Meanwhile, my mind was arguing with itself. I thought, "The reason I want to do this....Wait a minute! It's not that I want to do this, but for some reason, I *have* to do this."

The reason I finally gave myself for walking blindfolded was that I wanted to see, as an actor would, how I could expand my senses without using my eyes. I also wanted to prove that, if I put aside any fears I might have, people would not hurt me or take advantage of me.

So I set out for nine days traveling blindfolded, and during that time, I found that my senses really did expand. After a while, I could actually feel things through my skin!

And everyone I met was fantastic—even though I never saw their faces. I learned that I could trust people, even though I was "helpless." Maybe that's why they responded as they did. But each step I took as a blind man opened my eyes to how beautiful people really are.

BLISS

I started out from Boston with my eye patches on. On my third day out, I found myself standing for about six hours in one spot in western Pennsylvania. Nobody picked me up and I was so cold I thought I was getting frostbite. Finally, I couldn't take it any longer. I reached up to take my eye patches off, ready to give up. But when I touched them, I heard a deep voice say, "Stop! Don't give up. Keep doing what you're doing."

Somehow, I knew I had to obey the voice, so I lowered my hands. When I did, I suddenly felt that strange breeze again. But this time the calm it brought went far deeper than it had the first time. I was so full of bliss, I felt as if I was ready to explode. Then, I actually felt myself going out of my body.

It was incredible. Suddenly, there I was above my body, looking down at myself hitch-hiking. And for the first time, I knew we were more than just our bodies. As I watched myself from above, I saw a car drive up and offer me a ride.

Then I was back in my body. I must have looked pretty dazed as I got into the car. It was a mixture of amazement from what I had just experienced, and being near frozen.

TRUSTING

Altogether it took me nine days to get across the country. From Boston and Pennsylvania, I went on to Iowa and then to Texas to be a movie extra in Robert Redford's movie, "The Great Waldo Pepper."

It was really enjoyable to work on a movie. But when I left, I knew I had to put my patches back on. I kept heading towards California, always letting the drivers who picked me up start the conversation. Almost always, they would ask me how I had damaged my eyes.

I would say, "Well, I actually have my eyesight, but I'm doing an in-depth research study of our senses."

The reaction was always the same. The driver would say, "Are you crazy? Aren't you afraid someone will hurt you or hit you over the head?"

I always had the same answer: "Well, I want to prove to myself that if I'm not afraid, people won't give me anything to be afraid of."

"That's wonderful," they would say. "And it must be working."

It did work. I was never hurt or threatened while I was walking "sightless." I was always treated with kindness, caring and concern.

NOTHING TO FEAR

Speaking of concern,, a nice couple picked me up once and took me home. They were worried that I might be doing damage to my eyesight by keeping my eyes closed for such a long time. So they called their eye doctor, who warned me that I might develop what's called "ball sensation," the moving of the eyeball up into the socket.

I wasn't worried, though, because I knew deep inside that I was supposed to keep my eyes closed. And I never did have a problem with my eyeballs.

3

The Awakening

*Once we turn within, the truth
really does set us free.*

SPIRIT SPEAKS

I finally got to California and stayed with
friends in Los Angeles. Barbara and Sherm were
a couple I'd met back in the '60s, and they'd
offered me a standing invitation to stay with
them whenever I was in the area. They lived
near the Angeles Crest mountains.

Now, every day when I woke up, I felt a
powerful urge to walk up to the top of those
mountains. I knew that once I got there, I'd
begin to fast.

One day, after a couple of months, I did walk up to the top. Then, I fasted. For the first time, I really felt a oneness with the universe. I took off my clothes and let the sun shine down on me.

On the third evening of my fast, I felt great bliss, and it came to me that I was experiencing God. I asked, "What should I do?" And an inner voice said, "Start walking and be love, and no matter what anyone does, send them love."

"I will," I promised.

After I received this message, instructional wisdom just started flowing into me. Questions would form in my mind and instantly be answered. I learned that:

1. I wasn't to organize or join an organization.

2. I wasn't to go to others for answers. All the answers to my questions could be found within me.

3. I wasn't to be influenced by the written word.

I knew then that God's wisdom was in all of us. God wasn't something up in the clouds, or in the Bible, or even in a church. I also realized that we're here on this planet to become one with that Source, and for our bodies to connect with Spirit.

Later, when it was time to sleep, I got dressed and dug a hole. Then I curled up in my blanket and pulled the dirt in over me. It got pretty cold up in the mountains.

In the middle of the night, I started awake. A man was standing above me with a flashlight, silently looking down at me.

"Yes?" I asked, trying to wake up. I wondered where he'd come from, and what he wanted with me.

He told me he had been camping down below the mountains and saw a light, so he came up to investigate. When he got close to where I was resting, he said, "The light was over you, but when I got close to you, the light disappeared."

I started to get out of my blanket, taking my eyes off him for a moment. When I looked up again, he was gone.

BREATHING IN LOVE

I finally left the mountains. As I was walking back home to Barbara and Sherm's, I remembered a book I had once read. In the book were these words: "All love and understanding fill my heart. All love and understanding shine throughout the world."

I suddenly understood that I was to breathe to those words. When I inhaled, I was to breathe in the idea, "All love and understanding fill my heart." As I exhaled, I was to breathe out, "All love and understanding shine throughout the world."

I tried it, and I felt wonderful! By turning my thoughts to the love within, and then sending that love out, I was able to control my thoughts and my breath.

This new way of breathing made a big difference in my life. It helped me focus my energies so I could create the loving spirit I wanted in my life, and send it out to others.

Try it. Just think the words, "All love and understanding fill my heart." Then think the words, "All love and understanding shine throughout the world." Breathe with the words.

See how good it feels?

FIRST LESSON

After I got back to Barbara and Sherm's place, I wanted to share with them what I had experienced up in the mountains. But for some reason, they couldn't hear what I was saying. It was as if they were closed off from my words.

I learned an important lesson that day. Before I could tell others what I had learned, I had to live it first and be an example. Then, people would ask.

Patience, my dear ones.

PART 2

Sharing the Love

4

Following My Guidance

Be still and open up to pure love.

WAITING

For the next couple of months, I painted houses for my friend, Bill, in Hollywood. But what I was really doing was waiting for guidance on how I could carry out the promise I had made up in the mountains—to walk and to love others.

A few months later, I woke up one morning and realized that the beautiful feeling of bliss I'd been enjoying was gone. I was lying on the couch, and for some reason my eyes were drawn to the coffee table. On it was a magazine with the words "Unity" on the cover.

When I opened it up and started reading an article, I recognized that it held the same wisdom that had come to me when I was on top of the mountain. I turned to the back of the magazine and saw the name "Sue" and a Santa Monica address on it.

I had the feeling I was to walk to Santa Monica, so I got dressed and started on my way. It was the first time I had ever voluntarily walked 25 miles. (The last time had been in the Army).

When I got to Santa Monica, it was eight in the evening. And there, standing in front of the Unity Church, was Sue herself, talking to a small congregation!

As soon as I saw her, I knew she was meant to be a teacher for me. So I stayed in Santa Monica from Lent to Palm Sunday, taking some of Sue's classes. Everything I heard reinforced what I had already learned, but it was really exciting to hear these ideas from another human being.

I also knew that I would be guided to the next person and the next place on my journey. And so I waited.

TRUSTING THE VOICE

While I was at Unity, I heard about a healing seminar that was to be held in San Francisco, and I felt I was to attend the service. So the next day, I started walking to San Francisco.

It's funny, because sometimes we think we're headed somewhere for a certain reason. Then something happens along the way, and we realize that that was the real reason we were going in that direction.

This happened to me on my way to San Francisco. I passed a young woman who was collecting money, and when I turned back to look at her again, I saw, for the first time, another person's aura. It was white-gold, and the light was all around her. She was standing there in light looking so beautiful.

I asked the woman what she was collecting for and she said, "World happiness and understanding." Before I realized what I was doing, I had given her all the folded money I had in my right-hand pocket. Then I remembered that I only had 47 cents in my left pocket, and thought, "Uh, oh. I might need that money for food."

I started to reach for the money to take it back, when a voice said, "No. You will be provided for."

So I dropped my hands and walked away, leaving the woman with almost all my money. Suddenly, I felt as if 10,000 pounds had been lifted from me. The feeling of freedom that came to me then was indescribable.

At that moment, I knew I would always have enough. And it has been so. Now, over twenty years later, I am still walking, and Spirit is still providing.

THE VISITATION

Two years after I began walking and waving, I went to fast at Lake Mead, east of Las Vegas. It was during this fast that I truly found out why I was walking and waving.

On the thirteenth day of my fast, I had a "visitation." It was about three in the morning. I was asleep when I heard a deep voice saying, "You are the King. You are the King. You are the King of this Earth."

I remember thinking, "Am I asleep or awake?" Then, when I realized I was awake, I was astounded! I wondered, "How could I be King?" But then I realized that the voice wasn't just talking to me, it was talking to everyone. I guess I'd been able to tune into it because my vibration was so high from the fasting I'd done.

My eyes were still closed, and when I opened them, I saw a bright light in front of me—a glowing, shining white presence. The voice that seemed to be coming from this light continued speaking. "We are coming to an age of peace, and you come before Me to gather all people together as one. From this day on, you shall walk in My Name. "

Then, the most beautiful music I've ever heard started playing. It lasted for about an hour, and then it stopped. Just before dawn, the light presence went away, and I saw a ray of light that went to a star in the East.

For the next three days, I didn't know what to think. I knew what I had seen and heard, but I couldn't figure out how I was supposed to gather everyone together.

On the third day after the visitation, sounds came to me. The first was, "Kaieb" and then I heard the words, "The year 2003." I had no idea what "Kaieb" meant, but it sounded like a name, so I decided to call myself "Kaieb" for awhile.

Then, I was given to understand that 2003 would be The Year of Peace on Earth, and that I would be guided as to what to do next.

THE HEART STONE

Days and weeks and years went by. Each day brought me new lessons in loving. One day, I was walking up Highway 1 from Los Angeles to San Francisco when I passed a cemetery.

I had learned to follow my inner guidance, so I walked into the cemetery and was drawn to a grave where a baby had been buried that morning. I stood there looking at the site, and I felt such compassion that I found a heart-shaped stone and carefully laid it on top of the baby's headstone.

Years later, I was headed down to Los Angeles on Route 395 when an elderly lady picked me up near Lake Topago. After we talked for awhile, I gave her a stone. She said, "Let me tell you about a stone I found years ago. My little granddaughter had just died, and the day after her funeral, we took some flowers to lay on her grave. I found a heart-shaped stone on the headstone."

She said the family thought it was a sign from Jesus telling them that everything was all right. Then I told her, "I'm the man who put that stone there."

She just looked at me, unbelieving. Then, she reached for my hand, and I reached for hers, and we held hands and sobbed all the rest of the way.

SOFT RAIN

One day I was walking in Big Sur. It had just started drizzling, and as I was approaching a cliff, I saw a young woman standing at the top, looking out over the ocean. When she heard me walking up behind her, she turned with a start.

Her next words surprised me. "Where are you going?" she asked.

"San Francisco," I told her. To my surprise, she began to cry. So I asked her if she wanted to talk.

She told me she had just been ready to jump off the cliff when she had heard my footsteps. I then know why we had come together, and started talking to her about my path. Then, she opened up and shared her story with me.

I asked her if she wanted to spend the day together, and after she thought about it for a minute, she said, "Yes." So we got in her car and started going north. After a few miles, we saw a beautiful meadow and stopped the car. We got out and lay down on the soft green grass and talked some more. Then we reached out and made love.

We had a beautiful weekend together, and when we parted, she was at peace. As we hugged goodbye, she looked at me and said, "Now I can go back to my life."

DETOUR

One day, I lost my voice, and I got the message that I was supposed to be quiet for awhile. I kept on hitchhiking, and was directed by Spirit to go to Zion National Park in Utah.

After walking for a few days, I got to the center of Utah. A man picked me up and said he was going to San Diego—just the opposite direction from Zion National Park.

For some reason, I decided to accept his offer. I wrote down "OK" on my writing pad, and we took off.

The man asked me to drive, but I wrote a note saying that I had no license. "That's all right," he told me. "I'm really tired."

So I got behind the wheel, and two blocks later I crashed into a car that pulled in front of us. I dented our car's front fender and messed up the other car, and when the police came and learned I didn't have a license, they took us to the police station.

For some reason, I felt calm. I was sitting in the back seat of the police car, and the officer who was driving kept looking at me in the rear view mirror. Finally, he said, "Man, you have to be the happiest, most peaceful man I've ever arrested." I couldn't talk, but I smiled because I did feel peaceful.

When we arrived at the courthouse, we found out that the judge had just gone home. A woman who acted as clerk went in and got a big book.

"Are you guilty?" she asked me.

I nodded, "Yes."

"That'll be ten dollars," she said.

I thought she wanted a ten dollar deposit to make sure I'd come back later. So I wrote on my pad, "When do you want me to return?"

She said, "No. That's your fine."

Isn't that something? She fined me ten dollars for driving one car without a license, and wrecking the other one. She also fined the other guy ten dollars because he let me drive his car.

Boy, was he angry! I looked at him and wrote down on my pad, "Don't be angry. Everything is in Divine Order."

But that only got him angrier. He looked at me and said, "Oh, man, that's a lot of garbage. What are you, a religious nut?"

I said, "No. But I've come to help awaken the Christ in man."

He told me he didn't believe in that stuff, but I said, "That's all right. One day you will, because it's true."

I left the courthouse, but before I could get onto the highway, I saw the officer who arrested me talking with two other deputy sheriffs. As I walked up, I heard him say, "Here he comes now."

When I got up to him, he said, "I was just telling my friends here that I arrested the happiest man I've ever seen. Where's your friend?"

I wrote down on my pad, "He didn't realize he was my friend, and he got angry because I told him that everything was in Divine Order."

When the officer read that to his other two deputies, they all said, "Wow, yeah!" "Okay, yeah, " they kept saying.

So I sat down and wrote on my pad, "If Spirit is guiding us and tells us where to go, and if we don't follow that, we might have to get in a car wreck to get back on the right path."

5

Learning to Forgive

*If we are experiencing anything but peace
in the present, it's probably because
we haven't forgiven someone.*

TWO STORIES ABOUT "THE FINGER"

One day I was waving down in Arlington, Nevada and a guy across the street gave me the finger. That's happened before, so I walked over to talk to him to find out why he was so angry. As I walked up to him, he hit me on the chin.

I'd been hit a lot of times in my wild days, but this was one of the hardest blows I'd ever received. My knees almost buckled. I said, "I don't want to fight you. I'm here to share love."

The man just looked at me and shook his head. Then he walked away.

I was very upset by all this. For once, I didn't feel unconditional love coming from my heart. Instead, I sat down on the curb and cried. I felt like a little boy who'd had his candy stolen from him.

A tiny old lady who knew me from my walking came up to me and said, "Are you all right, Ed?"

I said, "Yes, but I've been walking all these years waving and sharing love, and that guy just hit me."

Then, a young man in a van stopped and asked if I was all right. I told him the same thing and he said, "Come on, I'll give you a ride."

As soon as I got in, he wanted to go after the guy and beat him up. I said, "No, let's just forgive him."

"How can you forgive him after he did that to you?" my new friend wanted to know. I told him that one of the ways we can have a happy life is by forgiving those who hurt us.

You know, twenty years earlier, I wouldn't even have hesitated to deck the man who hit me. I'm a strong man, and I used to fight a lot. It was my path at the time.

But now, I was more interested in forgiveness than in revenge. Isn't it amazing how our paths wind around, leading us in totally new directions?

————————

I had another opportunity to learn about forgiveness one day in Reno, Nevada.

Every so often, I'm asked to go on Reno's KOH Talk Show. One day when I was leaving the station, a man stopped me. He said, "Ed, do you have a couple of minutes?"

I said, "Sure," curious about what he had to say.

"I just want to let you know that for the last thirteen years, every time I saw you, I would give you the finger, even though I didn't know you," he admitted. "Then, if anyone was with me, I would tell them not to wave because you were nothing but a bum. But when I heard your story today, I wanted to tell you that I'm sorry I hated you so much. Today, I want to tell you that I love you."

Then he hugged me and started crying. There we were on the street, hugging each other and crying. This man had felt hate for thirteen years, and then heard words that turned his hate into love.

I love you all.

HEALING STARTS WITH YOU

A woman stopped me once. She wanted to talk, and knew it was safe to tell me what was bothering her. She said she was going to have to leave her husband because he had such a terrible temper, and she was beginning to have one, too.

I told her, "Well, you can leave him if you want to, but if you leave before you've found peace in this situation, down the road you're going to meet someone else with a temper."

She started laughing and said, "You know, you're right! My first three husbands had a temper!"

I decided to offer her this advice: "Every time you think of your mate, first say "thank you," because everyone we come in contact with is teaching us to find our true selves.

"Then say, 'I forgive you for the way you act. Forgive me for what I have been thinking about you.' Finally, say, 'All love and understanding fill my heart. All love and understanding shine throughout the world.' If you have to say this ten thousand times a day, do it, and it will work."

The woman nodded and agreed to try it. I don't know what happened to her, but I hope it worked. Another woman I suggested it to stopped me years later and said, "Your suggestion worked, Ed. We're still together."

I'm so happy when people tell me the good things that happen to them.

6

Learning to Receive

It takes as much love to receive
as it does to give.

THE UNIVERSE WILL PROVIDE

The first week I was walking, I didn't know I could be provided for without asking someone for help. So when I got to a town, I would go into the grocery store and ask for fruit and vegetables. Usually, I was given more than I could carry.

One day, I was asked to clean out a toilet to earn some food. So I did.

The next day, I was walking along when a highway patrolman stopped and asked me where I was going. I told him I was walking to San Francisco. We started to talk, and then we sat down and shared for about half an hour. He had some problems, and I offered what words I could to help him see them more lovingly.

Finally, we got up to go our separate ways. To my surprise, he said, "Here, take this," and handed me his lunch and seven dollars. And from that time on, things came to me without my having to ask for them.

I realize now that this was the beginning of my needs being filled by having loving thoughts. By sending love out to others, I would receive it back in the form I needed.

RECEIVING IS ITS OWN REWARD

In my first few years as "The Waver," when people wanted to give me things, I would usually say, "You don't have to do that. I'm not doing this for any reward."

Then, after about three years of waving, I was walking down to Smith Valley to speak to a Rotary Club. On the way there, a little old man in a pickup truck stopped and asked me if I would like a ride. I said, "No, thank you."

He said, "Please let me give you a ride." Again, I said, "No."

As he drove off, I saw him start to cry. When I saw his tears, I suddenly realized that I should be as open to receiving as I am to giving. If I stop receiving from someone, I shut off their natural flow of giving. And that's the last thing I want to do!

So from that day on, I've learned to become a great receiver, as well as a giver.

FOUND MONEY

I recall one time I was leaving Iowa after a visit with my former wife, Bonnie. She'd given me $5 to start out with.

I was headed for Los Angeles along Highway 30 when a driver threw a bill at me. I ran over and picked it up. It was a $10 bill.

The next man who picked me up said he was a born-again Christian. After awhile, he said he was really worried about his fiancée because she was not living a Christian life. He believed she was sinning.

I thought about this for a minute, and then I said, "You know what I've found out about sin? It's just another lesson we experience as we get to know God. The closer we come to God, the less we have to sin. Eventually, when we become one with God, we'll sin no more, and the lessons will be over."

Then, I said, "Why don't you just try to love her no matter what she's doing? Just love her unconditionally."

He was quiet for a few minutes, and then he agreed. "I've really been judging her. Well, from now on, I'm going to try not to judge her, and just love her."

Those words must have hit home, because after he said that, he looked at me in amazement.

"I can't believe it. I pick up a hitchhiker and you change my life. How can I help you get to Los Angeles?"

I answered, "Just do what your heart says."

"Would you like to have my car?" he offered. I thought he was joking, but no, he was serious. I was really moved by his offer, but I had to refuse him.

"No, that's not part of my life right now. If I'd had a car, I wouldn't have met you," I pointed out.

Then he asked how much money I'd need to get to Los Angeles, and I told him, "I can't set a price on what I'm doing. Just give me what your heart says."

We drove for another hour, and then it was time for him to drop me off. He said, "Ed, I've been listening to my heart, but it hasn't told me how much to give you."

So he took out his billfold and opened it up. Handing it over to me, he offered, "Here, take what you want. Take it all if you like."

I waited for guidance to tell me what to do. Then, I said, "I'll just take half." So I took about half of his money and put it in my pocket. He was happy and so was I.

Then, we hugged and said goodbye. When I reached the Interstate going into Des Moines, I took the money out and counted it. I had $900—three $100 bills and the rest were $50s!

That was a lot more money than I'd expected, but I figured it was with me for a reason. So I walked to the bus station in Des Moines and got a ticket, and then went out and had a nice dinner. I ate really well all the way to Los Angeles.

When I arrived at my friend Barbara's house, she opened the door and said, "Oh, Ed, I'm always so happy to see you, but I don't know what we're going to do. I've been sick and I'm flat broke."

I said, "No, we're not," and I pulled out the rest of the money.

Spirit knew I was going to need more this time.

BOOTS

I was walking along when a young boy on a bicycle stopped and asked where I was going. I told him, "San Francisco."

He said he lived in the next town off Highway 1, and if I stopped by his house, his mother would fix me lunch. He gave me directions to get to their home.

When I found the house, I knocked on the door and a woman answered. I told her how I'd met her son, and that he'd suggested I stop there for lunch.

She was a nice woman and invited me in. Then she fixed me two big ham and cheese sandwiches. As I was eating and telling her why I walk and wave, she looked down at my feet and saw that my shoes were worn out.

"Would you like a new pair of boots?" she asked. Her husband had a new pair of Red Wings he'd never worn because they didn't fit him. I pulled them on, and they fit me perfectly.

Both of us were happy that the boots fit. It was another lesson in how, if we're open, Spirit will guide us to the right place and the right person when we're in need.

There really is no separation between all of us, even if we do seem to be "strangers."

WHAT GOES AROUND ...

One day, a doctor from India picked me up. We spent the whole day together, talking and sharing. Finally, just before he dropped me off, he said, "Ed, I'm a doctor and well-educated. Yet I pick up a hitchhiker and learn so much that will help me with my life. How can I repay you?"

I realized that to refuse him would deny him his right to give back. So I said, "Do whatever your heart says to do."

He thought a minute. "Well, I don't have any cash on me. Would you take my watch?"

I looked it over. It was a beautiful, expensive watch, and it had everything on it. What a gift from Spirit for sharing loving thoughts! "Thank you," I said, accepting the watch.

After I left him, I continued walking for awhile. The next people who picked me up were three young men on their way to work at a Denver hospital. After awhile, one of the men said he didn't know what he was going to do. His watch had broken that morning.

I said, "Well, take this one."

He looked at my new watch and said, "No, Ed," he said. "I can't take this. It's too expensive."

I said, "Yes, you can. Somebody gave it to me this afternoon. Now I'm giving it to you."

All this happened fifteen years ago. About three years ago, a friend of mine gave me a watch. When I looked at it closely, I couldn't believe it. It was just like the one I had given away in Denver.

It took twelve years for the spirit of that gift to come full circle back to me.

GAINING BY GIVING

I remember one time, I was speaking at a church. I'd left Reno with no money, but by the next week, I had $600 in my pocket—just from people opening their hearts and offering it to me.

After my speech, a woman came up, and I could sense she needed some money. So I gave her $40.

A man was standing nearby. He hadn't seen me give the woman the money, but when I turned around, he reached out and gave me $80, just like that. Obviously, the spirit of sharing was strong that day!

Another time, I was arrested in Flagstaff for waving. When I was released, I was approached by an Indian who was being released at the same time. He asked if I had any money. Although I only had $10, I gave it all to him. I wasn't worried. I knew the Universe takes care of us all.

Then, I started hitchhiking. The very first person who picked me up on the road offered me $20. The lesson keeps coming back—whenever we share what we have, it's returned to us, and then some.

7

Meditation, Visions, and Past Lives

If I hadn't been meditating,
I wouldn't have been able to do
what I've done all these years.

SEVEN BEINGS OF LIGHT

Years ago, when Gerald Ford was still President, I was meditating in a friend's home. Seven men in white robes appeared before me. I went to each one of them, and each said, "I am pure light." Then, I kissed the hands of the seventh one, and he said, "You are pure light."

Then, the beings told me nonverbally that I was to go to the heads of governments and tell them that the time of peace was coming.

I accepted all of this without question, and I was so anxious to get started, I immediately began hitchhiking to Washington, D.C.

Once I got there, I went to the mail room at the White House every day to leave a message for the President. At night I would sleep in a sleeping bag in the bushes behind Lincoln Memorial. Finally, hearing nothing from President Ford, I gave up.

Before I started back home to Reno, I wrote a note to the President and told him I was leaving now, but that I would return. When I dropped the note off at the mail room, one of the clerks told me that Special Agent so-and-so wanted to talk with me.

A young man came over and asked me why I wanted to harm the President. I told him I wasn't there to harm him, but to share the love I feel. Then he asked me what I knew about firearms, etc. I kept giving him the same answer.

Finally, I said, "I'm not going to answer any more questions because of the fears you have." He looked at me, speechless for a minute, and then told me I was free to go. I decided to come back when the fear was gone.

Later, I understood what had happened. Spirit had given me the right message, but my ego had made me rush out to Washington at the wrong time—several years too early.

I'll go back again when Spirit tells me the time is right.

HEART-TO-HEART COMMUNICATION

Once, just before entering Omaha, Nebraska, I had the feeling that a couple I knew down in Unity Village, Missouri wanted to talk with me. Because I was on the highway, at the Iowa/Nebraska border, I decided to send them thoughts of love and understanding, and the message that everything would be all right.

A short time later, I found myself crossing the road and going down to Missouri. I got to Unity Village a few days later, and the first person I saw was the wife of the couple that I felt wanted to talk to me. She was very relieved to see me.

Apparently, she was having a hard time. She and her husband were getting a divorce, and she asked if I'd come over to her house that evening to sit and talk with her. I said I would.

When I got there, I led her in a special meditation that's very helpful for people going through rough times. After we finished she said, "A couple of nights ago, I was lying in bed crying and needing to talk to you. Then you appeared at the foot of my bed and smiled. You said, 'Everything is going to be all right.'"

She had received my message at the same time I'd sent it from Iowa. Time and place offer no barriers to loving words.

A GLIMPSE OF OTHER LIFETIMES

My friend, Richard, taught nonverbal communication and drama. The moment we met, we felt as if we were long-lost brothers. One day, his drama class put on "Godspell."

I was sitting in the front row, right on the aisle, watching the play and really enjoying it. All of a sudden, I found myself back in the days of Jesus. I was Judas, and I saw myself running and screaming in fear. Then, I jumped off a cliff to my death.

The next thing I was aware of, I was sitting there in my seat sobbing, with the whole cast around me, patting me and trying to console me.

I know that, according to the Bible, Judas hung himself. But later I found out that some Bible scholars are questioning this.

In other past-life recalls, I've seen myself as an American Indian preparing for battle, and as an African raiding villages. I hadn't been sure I believed in past lives before these experiences, but now I do.

JUDAS #1

One day I was reading *I, John*, by Ben Lewis, a book my friend Carol Coe had given me. Ben felt he was the reincarnation of John, the Beloved, the youngest disciple. When I was reading the book, I had a vision of myself as Judas in an olive garden, talking with John.

After that experience, I said to myself, "I have to talk to this Ben." I found out he lived near Washington, DC, so I set out to find this man who might be able to shed some light on the day I had seen myself as Judas.

Of course, this was going against the guidance I had received—to seek the truth only from within, and not from anyone else. But my curiosity was too strong to miss the opportunity to meet Ben Lewis.

When I got to Washington, I found out where he lived. As I walked up to the front door, I was surprised to see bars over all the windows and the door.

I knocked on the door and a lady answered it, with a little old man standing behind her. I said, "Hi, my name is Kaieb and I come in the name of the Lord."

Both of them immediately said, "Go on, get out of here."

I said, "Wait, I'm a friend of Carol Coe's."

Then the old man, who was Ben, said, "Oh, yes, I've talked to her many times about The Golden Scripts. Come on in."

I ended up staying for a week with Ben and his wife. Oddly, we never talked about why I had come. Instead, while I was at Ben's, I mopped their floors and sprayed for cockroaches every day. I knew there was a reason I was doing this, so I waited to find out what it was.

The day before I left, Ben said, "Ed, sit down. You know, twenty-five years ago when I wrote, *I, John,* I was living the love that you're living. But things happened and I became bitter, fearful, and a real bigot. Then you came into my life and you truly 'de-bugged' us. You got the bugs out of our house, and the bugs out of me.

"I know I'm about to pass from this body, but one thing has to happen first. In this incarnation, I've met all the disciples except Judas. I want to meet Judas before I pass."

I said, "I'm here now."

He threw his arms around me and started crying. "Now, I can go," he said.

JUDAS #2

A few years went by. I was in Salt Lake City staying with my friend, Ed. One day, we went to a picnic sponsored by Unity and Science of Mind churches. Two ladies came up and asked if they could eat with us. "Of course," we said.

After we ate and talked awhile, one of them suddenly asked me, "Which one are you?"

I knew immediately what she was talking about, and said, "I am the one they called 'The Betrayer' and now I come to spread light in the world today." I could hardly believe the words that had come out of my mouth, but the women accepted them without a second thought, and we continued our earlier conversation.

Another year passed, and it kept coming to me that the two women I had met that day had a message for me. So the next time I went through Salt Lake City, I looked them up.

They were so happy to see me, and told me they'd been waiting for me. Both of them had a talent for automatic writing, and they said they had been communicating with Jacob from the Bible.

The day they had met me, they both went home to their apartments and separately asked Jacob the same question: "Is the man we met today in the park who he says he is?"

They both got the same answer. It was all typed out in their journals. The answer was, "Yes, he was Judas, the one they called 'The Betrayer' during the time of Jesus Christ. And he now comes to spread the light in the world today."

I felt such joy when I heard those words. Another piece of the puzzle of my life had fallen into place.

ALMOST BEYOND BELIEF

I had another experience that really shook me. It happened about a year after my past-life recall at the play, "Godspell."

As I was hitchhiking past a ranch, I was watching kids playing in the yard. Suddenly, something told me to look up, and coming right at me was a white pickup truck. Before I could jump out of the way, it hit me and passed through the right portion of my body, as if I were transparent.

I couldn't believe what had happened—it just took my breath away. But at that moment, I was filled with a sense of "knowing" Jesus and Buddha. It's hard to explain, but I could *feel* who they had been. I also knew that they had come to show us that through love, we can transcend everything, even physical death.

It took a few minutes for me to recover, and I remember thinking, "I'm a storyteller, but I'm not going to be able to tell this one to anyone. Nobody will believe this story."

Then it came to me that when we truly get to a point of loving others unconditionally, we stop worrying about whether or not they'll believe us. We just tell our truth as we know it.

CAROL

After I had I pulled myself together from being "hit" by the white truck, I went back to hitchhiking. The next person to stop to pick me up was a woman. Her name was Carol Fuller, and when I looked in her eyes, I knew she would believe me if I told her what had just happened. So I did, and I was right: she totally accepted my experience.

Two weeks later, Carol was driving along and saw me hitchhiking. She stopped the car and handed me a book she'd been holding onto, hoping we'd see each other again.

She told me she had never been able to read this book until she met me. Then she had gone home and opened it up to the page that read:

"We are coming to an age of peace, and there will be a red-haired man walking along the roadside waving that will help bring us all together as one."

This was written in 1952 by a woman called Pensatia. I was only 15 at the time, and it was years before I had begun walking and waving. When I read this page, I said, "My God, this woman was writing about me."

A MESSAGE FOR ED

One day after I'd spoken to a Unity Church group, I had a surprise. I've spoken to groups hundreds of times over the years, and I've told my stories and shared my chants.

This time, after my talk, a man came over to me and said, "I just want to tell you how beautiful and pure your chants and stories are. You know, part of your chant is from Sanskrit. 'Ka Re Rom' means 'bringing forth pure energy.'"

I said, "Really! Isn't that exciting!" I never know what these sounds mean when they come from within me. But his words just confirmed for me that all wisdom truly does dwell within us.

THE MIRROR

From time to time, people stop me and tell me their stories. One couple, Betty and Dick, told me about an amazing mirror that gave them messages. Dick had been going through a depression. One day, he was in tears and asked God, "If you're really there, please give me a sign."

He was in the bathroom when all this happened, and he looked up to see an imprint that had formed on his bathroom mirror. It was circular and had marks where eyes, nose and a mouth would be. It didn't look human, but it did resemble a mask of some sort.

Eventually, Betty and Dick asked a para-psychologist to come in and give his opinion of what the image meant. When the man arrived, he looked at the imprint on the mirror very carefully. Then he told the couple that he knew of a handful of other cases like this. His theory was that the image was that of a spirit that had never been in a body.

So the couple communicated by ouija board with this image, and they called it "Shasta." Now, they said, Shasta wanted to talk to me.

I wasn't sure I wanted to get involved in this, but I did agree to come over when it felt right. I'm pretty open to everything, but I must admit I had my doubts about Shasta.

That night, I kept getting the feeling I should go see Shasta. The next morning when I woke up, it was the same thing—Shasta. So I went, just to find out why I was being urged to see this image on the mirror.

When I got to their home, Betty and Dick took me to see the mirror. Sure enough, there it was, all encased in wood on the wall. And on the mirror was a strange image.

The couple started to tell me about Shasta, but I said, "No, don't tell me anything yet. Just let me sit here and see what happens."

So I sat down in front of Shasta and began to chant. What happened next was amazing. All wisdom and understanding came forth from the mirror and welled up inside of me, and tears of joy began streaming down my face. What I experienced was truly beyond words. I must have sat there in front of that mirror for about an hour.

Finally, just before I finished chanting, Shasta gave me a message for Betty and Dick. I gave it to them right away.

"Before you say anything," I told them, "I have a message for you from Shasta. Shasta told me to tell you to stop using the ouija board. Be patient, and Shasta will communicate with you without the board."

They laughed and said, "Yes, Shasta told us the same thing through the board. But we haven't been ready to try to talk to Shasta without it."

Just to show me how they did communicate with Shasta, they went to the ouija board, and I've never seen any two people work it so fast. The first thing that came through was K-A-I-E-B. They asked me, "What is Kaieb?" I told them it was a sound that had come to me while I was fasting at Lake Mead.

Betty and Dick than told me that Shasta wanted to thank Kaieb for what he was doing, and to keep following the light.

And I am.

8

Teaching and Healing

The power is within us all.

GURU

Many years ago, I was walking up to Virginia City to spend the weekend with a friend. A young lady came walking up behind me. She told me her name was Joy, and said, "Can I talk with you?"

Then she told me that she had been living in a spiritual commune over in California, and that people there had been talking about me. And it came to her that I was to be her guru.

I asked Joy what she felt a guru was, and she said, "A teacher."

I said, "My dear, I'm not here to be followed. Your teacher is dwelling within you. Seek that teacher within and you will have to search no more."

Joy was disappointed, but she thanked me and went on her way. I've found that so many people are looking for answers in others, yet the truth is inside each one of us. All we need to do is to look there, and to listen.

THE TOWN DRUNK AND
THE SHOESHINE BOY

All through my life, I have met wonderful teachers. I know that everyone is a teacher as well as a student. As I reflect back on my life, I realize that I've learned something from everyone I've met.

But my first and most important teachers were the town drunk and the shoeshine boy. I met these wonderful men when I was in my early teens in Burlington, Iowa.

What did I learn from them? These two men taught me not to judge by appearances. The more I saw them, the more I realized that I loved spending time with them. Despite their situations, both men were, in their own way, wise and understanding. They totally accepted who they were—they knew their weaknesses, but they still loved themselves. There wasn't any shame or embarrassment for their past or present circumstances.

Of all the teachers I've had over the years, those two men have stayed in my mind and my heart.

YUKTSWAR

For years, a man appeared to me from time to time—sometimes in meditation, sometimes when I was awake. He was an old, white-haired man, and I always saw him in a lying-down position.

The old man never said a word, but just smiled. Whenever he appeared, I would walk up to him and just look down at that smile of his. When I did, great wisdom came through him and into me.

I never knew who this white-haired man was until a few years ago, when someone I knew stopped me while I was waving and gave me a book.

"Happy Birthday," my friend said. I looked at the title and smiled. It was *Autobiography of a Yogi*. The funny thing is, for years people had said to me, "I read this book and I thought of you. It's a book you've just got to read."

So I looked at my birthday present and said, "Well, I guess it's time." I opened it up and read some, and pretty soon I got to the part about a spiritual teacher named Yuktswar, and there was a picture of him. Sure enough, it was the white-haired smiling man I'd been seeing all these years.

It's strange, but after I read the book, he never appeared to me again. I missed seeing him, and one day, I thought, "Yuktswar has never appeared again. I sure would like to see him."

Well, the next best thing happened. About five minutes after that thought came, the same man who gave me the book drove by. When he saw me, he stopped and handed me a picture of Yuktswar.

Thank You. Thank You. Thank You.

42ND STREET STORIES

Once, when I was in New York, I went into a theater on 42nd Street. I was sitting there when a security guard came up to a guy who was asleep and said, "Wake up!" As he spoke, he hit him in the foot.

The man woke up, angry, and started wrestling with the guard. Then a couple of people who worked in the theatre wrestled him up to the lobby. By now, other people who were watching the movie were going to the man's defense. As I walked into the lobby, it looked as if a riot was about to start.

People were getting excited, and I knew we were in for trouble. But most of all, I knew I wanted to calm down the man who'd been sleeping, so I walked right up to him through the crowd and said, "Everything's gonna be all right."

That was it. For some reason, he believed me, and he quieted right down. Everybody else started to walk away.

A city policeman had been called in to prevent a riot from starting. He came up to me and said, "I've been on the force for 20 years, and I've never seen anything like that. You just stopped a riot. What did you do?"

I said, "I just walked up to him and I shared positive energy and love, and he felt that. The positive energy helped heal his anger."

The policeman just shook his head and walked away. But I knew that Spirit had drawn me to that theater for that very reason.

———

Another time, I was walking down 42nd Street with Jack, a friend of mine who was a professor at New York University. On our way to dinner, we passed lots of "street people." Finally, when we had sat down in a Greek restaurant, Jack looked at me and said, "Ed, you're amazing."

I didn't understand. "Why do you say that?" I asked.

He said, "I'm sitting here looking at you and your eyes are just aglow. You look as peaceful and as happy as you did when we left the apartment. And I feel all depressed because of all the poor souls we just passed on 42nd Street."

I said, "You know what happened as we walked down 42nd Street, Jack? You were reacting to what you saw, and I was sending them love."

When we're truly sending love, we don't react to what we see. Then, we begin to understand that we're all on our own journeys to find out about life and about Spirit.

EGO

We're often told that "ego" is a bad thing—it's the selfish part of us that can sometimes be destructive to ourelves and others. In fact, I've had people tell me that our egos must die before the God within us can be born. But I just don't go along with that.

I think ego can be a good thing sometimes. When a girl in the Midwest told me that she believed pride was a sin, I said, "Oh, dear, be proud of yourself. You're part of God. To reject your ego is to reject God."

If we are of God, which I believe to be true, we should allow ourselves to feel both humble and proud. Humble that we're able to experience our beautiful lives and God's love, and proud to be a part of God. In that way, we'll be in perfect balance.

CROSSING PATHS

I was walking south of Monterey, California on Highway 1. This has got to have one of America's most beautiful views. As I walked, I was looking out over the ocean. The highway was closed to traffic because of mudslides.

Then, I heard footsteps. Two men I'd seen twice before were about to pass by. This time, I said, "Come on, sit down and talk awhile. This is the third time we've crossed paths. There must be something more to this."

They stopped, and I said, "My name's Ed," and put my hand on one man's shoulder. For some reason, I left it there a minute or two.

"My God," he cried. "You've just healed me!"

"What do you mean?" I asked, surprised. He sure didn't look sick to me, and I've never really considered myself a healer.

He explained, "Well, I have bronchitis, and I haven't been able to breathe through my nose for years. But the minute you touched me, I could breathe freely."

"Oh!" I said. "So that's why we were to meet!"

When we reach out in love, anyone can be a healer.

9

Wishes Do Come True

The power of thought is almost as powerful as the power of no thought.

THE FISH POND

One day, many years ago, I was visiting a friend in North Hollywood. While I was there, I offered to dig a big fish pond for him. I got started, but it was pretty hard work for one man.

On the second day I was digging, I noticed that a big machine across the street was digging a ditch. I thought, "Gee, it would be nice if that guy would come over and dig out this hole for me."

About twenty minutes later, the man who was digging the ditch came over and said, "Hey, I'm on my break, and I've been watching you dig this hole. Would you like me to do it? It will only take me 15 or 20 minutes."

Would I! I smiled and said, "That would be great."

When my friend came home that night, the pond was dug. He couldn't believe it. He asked me, "How did you manage that?"

"It was the power of thought," I answered, looking mysterious. But there isn't really any mystery about how a thought can become a reality.

Because we are all part of the Creator, we, too, have the power to create. And we do, every day, with the thoughts we think. That's why it's so important to keep our thoughts positive and loving, so our lives can become that reality.

THE GOOD SAMARITAN

Years ago, I was hitchhiking in Mississippi. Usually, I get rides pretty fast. But this day, I had gone about six hours without a ride. It was cold and raining, and I was soaked clear through. I was starting to feel angry. When the next car passed me, I threw up my arms and swore at it.

As soon as I did that, I had a vision of the Good Samaritan. I then understood that it was all right to pass someone by, and it was also all right to be passed by. Both of these situations were lessons in acceptance for us.

As soon as I had this vision, the car that had passed me turned around and came back. The man who was driving said, "Get in, brother. We were going to pass you, but when we saw you throw your hands into the air, I saw a picture of the Good Samaritan and I couldn't pass you by."

I said, "I saw the same vision," and his wife said, "Thank you, Jesus."

So I started telling them my story. After awhile, the husband asked me what they could do for me, and I said, "I would love to have a dry place to sleep."

So they took me home and we had a great dinner. The next day, when the husband took me out to the highway to drop me off, we stood there hugging and crying. It felt as if we were lifelong friends saying goodbye.

I don't remember your name, my brother, but you truly are my lifelong friend.

DON'T TRY SO HARD

When Bonnie and I were in Germany soon after we got married, we wanted a child. After awhile, when she didn't get pregnant, we took all kinds of tests to find out what was wrong. The doctors couldn't find anything, but finally we gave up and started talking about adopting. Shortly afterward, Bonnie got pregnant with our first daughter, Theresia.

I guess that happens a lot when we try so hard, and there's so much anxiety around what we want. It just doesn't happen.

It's the same with hitchhiking. Over the years, I've learned that any time I was anxious about getting a ride, no one would stop. As soon as I lost my anxiety, someone would pick me up.

As soon as we lose our anxiety about getting there—we're there!

DRUGSTORE GLASSES

Let me tell you how I found Eric, my eye doctor. Years ago, somebody asked me to look at a football card and pick some winners. I was wearing a pair of glasses that my friend, Betty, had bought for me at the drugstore. So when I read, I had to use a magnifying glass in addition to the glasses.

"Why don't you get a new pair of glasses?" my friend asked. As I walked out the door, I said, "I will."

I found myself heading for a bar called The Peppermill, and when I got there, I went straight to the gaming section. A man walked up to me and said, "My name is Eric. You probably don't remember me, but I heard you on a local radio show about ten years ago when I was a disc jockey."

"I remember,"I said. "You came out of a back room while I was on the show."

"Well, since that time, I've become an eye doctor, and I would like to get you some new glasses," he offered.

So he became my eye doctor.

Later, Eric introduced me to his friend, Nick, the sweetest and gentlest dentist I've ever known. Nick offered me free dental care. I felt so blessed. Sometimes, being The Waver can bring unexpected benefits!

HOME IS EVERYWHERE

A few years ago, I was staying with friends in Reno. I'd been there for several months when I became aware that it was time to move on. I asked Daniel, my chiropractor, if he knew anywhere I could live. It was the first time since I'd been waving that I asked someone ahead of time for a place to stay.

Daniel offered me an office in the back that he didn't use, and I lived there for another six months.

One morning, the cleaning lady saw me. Daniel was afraid she'd call the insurance people and tell them he had a tenant, which wasn't allowed. I went waving that day, and asked myself, "Am I supposed to stay in Reno?

Then, I told myself, "If somebody doesn't come and offer me a place to stay today, I will walk out of Reno."

About twenty minutes later, a woman stopped me. Her name was Najima, and she was from India. She said I had talked to her about three years earlier and helped her through a trying time. We talked awhile, and she looked down at her cassette player and took my tape out of it. "This tape is fantastic, Ed," she said. "I listen to it all the time."

She said she and her husband, Jay, had been listening to it only this morning, and they had agreed, "Wouldn't it be great if 'The Waver' could come live with us?"

I said, "I can. I have to leave the place where I've been living."

So that evening, Jay and I picked up my things and we went to their beautiful home on the north side of Reno. I stayed there for about six months, and we had a wonderful time together. Then I went back to Iowa to stay with my family for awhile.

People sometimes ask me how I feel about living with strangers. My answer is always the same: " I love it. Wherever I'm living at the time feels like home until I leave."

10

Jailhouse Stories

When we experience anger, it is almost impossible to see love.

WHERE'S YOUR I.D.?

I was traveling through Kansas once when it came to me that I was going to be arrested that day. Sure enough, I was waving in the next town when a deputy sheriff pulled me over. I said to myself, "Well, here goes."

The deputy asked me if I was bothering people. I said, "You know, I haven't talked to one person in this town. But if my waving and sharing the love I feel is bothering anyone, I guess I'm bothering the hell out of them."

He loooked at me for a few seconds. Then he started laughing. "Yeah, I guess you are bothering the HELL right out of them." So he allowed me to go on my way.

The next town I hit that day was Topeka. I waved through Topeka, and was just getting to the east side of the town when two policemen stopped and asked me for my I.D.

I told them that years ago, I had walked into the desert and torn up all my I.D. and thrown the pieces into the wind. As I saw them blowing away, I realized that I wasn't supposed to identify myself through paper anymore.

This story made them mad, and they kept getting angrier because I was being so peaceful. After I gave them my social security and other numbers verbally, I said, "Now, let me tell you why I walk and wave." But they didn't want to listen to what I was saying.

They told me to move away from them, so I started to walk away. Then they yelled at me to come back, and put handcuffs on me, really tight. "You're under arrest," they told me.

When they were booking me, one of the deputies said, "I suppose you think we're a bunch of rednecks, huh?"

I said, "No, I think you're children of God."

Then, I turned to the lady who was doing the booking. Tears were rolling down her cheeks.

LOVE OPENS THE JAILHOUSE DOOR

I was taken into a cell by a deputy. In a mocking voice, he yelled to the prisoners, "Here's Jesus to save you all." A black man was standing there, and he said in a serious voice, "Oh, I've been praying for you to come."

I laughed and said, "I'm not Jesus, but I have come to help you if you want it."

So we talked a bit. Then, the deputies came and put me in a cell with another man. I just sat quietly on the bunk for almost an hour, and finally the prisoner came up to me and said, "Hey, man, are you crazy or something?"

I said, "Why do you ask?"

He answered, "Well, you've been sitting there for almost an hour and you're just smiling. Don't you realize you're in jail?"

I told him, "I found out something a few years ago that allows me to be happy wherever I am."

For some reason, this made him angry, and he drew back his fist to hit me. "I found out something, too. It's you white bastards who got me in here."

He started to swing, but I looked him in the eye and said, "I love you, brother. Where I'm coming from, there is no skin color."

When I said that, he dropped his hand and walked back to his bunk. About ten minutes later, he started sobbing. "Please help me, please help me. I'm forty-eight years old and I've spent over half my life in prison. I love people, too, but I keep finding myself behind bars."

I felt his despair, and I told him gently, "One of the things I've found out is that each of us is on our own path to find God. Once you find your inner truth, you will never be imprisoned again. It's been your path to find that truth behind bars. When you do find it, the truth will set you free."

I asked him why he was back in prison this time. He said he had gotten out three days ago, but was immediately re-arrested for outstanding warrants against him while he'd been in jail.

I said, "By law those warrants should have been handled while you were still in jail."

He said, "Well, they weren't, and now I have to go back to jail."

Some of the other prisoners joined in, saying, "Yeah, he's going back."

But I wasn't so sure of that. I said, "Wait a minute. Let's change your thought processes a little." I asked the prisoner what he thought of the judge who was going to sentence him the next day.

He said, "That bastard is going to send me back to jail."

"My brother," I said, "realize that the judge you're going to see tomorrow and everyone you've ever met and will meet is a child of God. See him in that light."

"Now," I continued, "let's say this together: 'All love and understanding fills our hearts.' And then say to the judge, 'All love and understanding fills your heart.'"

I added, "You don't have to love him right now, just say the words."

So, for the next three or four hours, that's what we did.

By the time they took us to court the next day, this prisoner was a man at peace with himself.

As it turned out, we were the first to go before the judge. My friend went first and told the judge everything that had happened the night before. The judge asked him what he would do if he was free to go. My friend answered, "A gospel group has been wanting me to join them, and if you set me free, I'll call them up and join it."

The judge thought for a minute, and then said, "You're free to go."

My friend turned around in the courtroom, looked me in wonderment and said, "It works! Love truly works!"

I was the next and last man to be tried. The judge looked at me apologetically and said, "I'm sorry we've had to detain you. You're also free to go."

MORE I.D. STORIES

I was down in New Mexico, and it was about three o'clock in the morning. I was walking along, feeling such peace within myself, when a policeman stopped me and asked where I was coming from. I said, "Back there."

He said, "Where are you headed?" and I said, "Up there," pointing ahead.

He said, "Let me see your I.D."

I said, "I am who you're looking at."

He was a Native American, and I could see that he sensed the peace within me. I wasn't being a wise guy; I was just giving him simple answers. The policeman thought for a minute, and then chuckled. "Go on about your way."

I truly have been "going on about my way" these last twenty-two years. But the more I go on about my way, the more I know that we are all on the same path. Some of us just don't know it yet.

I was walking through Flagstaff, Arizona one day when a policeman stopped me. The first thing he asked me was whether I had any dope or weapons on me. I told him, "No, my life is to share the love I feel."

But he never did hear what I said about sharing the love I feel. He took my bag and dumped it out, and then searched me. Then he asked me for my papers. Of course, I had none. So he asked me for my social security number, and I gave it to him verbally. He wrote it down, and then asked for it again.

I said, "I told you my life is to share the love I feel, and I don't lie."

His reply was, "You're under arrest."

So there I was again, sitting in the back seat of a police car, handcuffed. The policeman said, "You know, the reason you're under arrest is because of your attitude."

I said, "No, the reason I'm under arrest is because of your fear. You're so into fear you can't see the love I'm sharing with you."

Of course, that was just the outer reason. The real reason I was arrested was to learn whatever lesson was waiting for me.

When I got to jail, I found out they had just held court. That meant I was going to be in jail until Monday. I sat in the jail cell, feeling so at peace I thought for sure I'd disappear out of that cell. Just as I thought I was going to disappear, the jailor opened up the cell door and yelled, "I don't know what's goin' on. They've never done this before, but they're holding special court for you."

When I got to court, I saw that the judge was a woman. She was so open to what I was saying, it was as if I was talking to someone who had invited me to come in especially to speak to her. I noticed she had quite a cough, and I suggested how she might get rid of it.

When I finished my story, she said, "That's beautiful, Ed. Keep doing what you're doing, and you're free to go." As I was leaving the courtroom, she put up both hands in a peace symbol and said, "Peace, my brother."

Love truly can set us free.

LOVE IN THE COURTROOM

I was back on Highway 1. This time I was waving just south of Santa Monica, California when two policemen gave me a ticket for hitchhiking. While one of them was writing it out, he said, "You probably won't pay this ticket, anyway."

"No," I admitted.

He started laughing and said, "You have to be the happiest, most peaceful man I've ever given a ticket to."

I gave the policeman my Iowa address, and by the time I returned there, a letter from a California court was waiting for me. It said there was a warrant out for me because I hadn't paid the ticket.

I wrote a letter explaining that my life is not a life of making money, but of sharing the love I feel and doing whatever I can to help people be happy. So I wished they would take this into consideration.

The next time I returned to Iowa, there was another letter from the court. But this one was from the judge, personally. It said, "This doesn't happen too often, but there is love in the courtroom today. Your fine is suspended."

Thank you, Judge! Thank you, Love!

WHY NOT FORGIVE?

I was hitchhiking just south of Salt Lake City one day when a highway patrolman stopped and asked for my I.D. When I told him I didn't have any, he whipped out a pair of handcuffs and put them on me. I told him that usually when I'm stopped, I explain what I'm doing in my life, and the police let me go.

But this patrolman said, "I don't want to hear any stories. The only thing I know is that if I stop somebody and they don't have an I.D., I wonder where he's just escaped from."

We arrived at the courthouse, but the judge was just leaving. He was a kind man, though, and said he would hear my case. First, he asked me if I was guilty of having no I.D. As usual, I said "yes." Then I told him my story.

After I finished explaining, he asked me if I had any money. When I said "No," he thought for a minute, and then in an apologetic voice, said, "I'm sorry, I'm going to have to send you to jail."

I said, "That's all right. You have to do what you have to do."

"But I don't want to send you to jail," he admitted, looking unhappy.

So I suggested, "Why don't you do what Jesus did. Forgive me."

The judge got a big smile on his face and said, "All right, my friend. I forgive you. You're free to go."

11

From Fear to Love

The more we are in the world and not of it,
the more we become the light of the world.

NAME-CALLING

It was about 2AM in Kansas, and I was hitch-hiking along the road when a car full of young men picked me up. They turned out to be brothers.

I had a beard and long hair at the time, and as soon as I got in, they started calling me names. They kept this up for an hour. Then, one of the brothers turned around and said, "We've been calling you all kinds of names and treating you really badly, and you just keep treating us nice. How come?"

So I told them what I did in life, and how I wanted to share love with everybody. After we talked for awhile, they ended up taking me home, where I spent the night. The next morning, their mother fixed us all a big breakfast and made me a couple of sandwiches to take with me.

I think all of us learned something that night. The lesson for me was one I keep learning over and over again. Life is a lot more peaceful when we don't react to others, no matter how they behave.

CHICAGO

I remember one night I was walking through the south of Chicago at around three in the morning. There's something like a murder a night in this area, and I was on Highway 30 going east when two officers stopped me. They were concerned that I might get mugged or beaten up.

"Don't you know where you are?" they asked me, looking worried.

"Yes," I answered. "I'm headed east."

"You know, you could get your throat cut in this neighborhood," one of the officers warned me. He looked as if he wasn't very happy being there, either.

But I wasn't worried. "No, I won't," I said. "I'm here to share love, and nobody can harm that."

The two policemen just laughed when I said that. Then they took off.

Soon after this, a man stopped and picked me up, and I told him what had just happened. He just laughed and said, "Those cops think we're gonna kill everybody." Then, we had a good talk, and he dropped me off.

Especially when I'm traveling, I stay with that love, stay with that light. Then there's nothing to fear.

SKIDDING

A man picked me up in Wyoming. After awhile, he asked me to drive for a bit. We began talking about fear, and he asked me how I felt about it, especially since I was on the road all the time.

I told him I believe that fear is just another lesson we experience on our paths to becoming one with God. The more we are filled with love, the less room there is for fear.

Right after we began talking about this, I drove around a curve and found us suddenly in the middle of a blizzard. At the same time, the car went into a spin. We must have spun around a dozen times, finally coming to a stop about fifty feet off the road in a snowbank.

The man I was with was shaking with fear. Looking over at me, he said, "I can't believe it. I was scared to death, and I looked over at you driving, and you were just as peaceful as if you were driving down a road that was all clear."

That experience for me was a reminder that I always have to live what I speak. Then, when I'm asked, I can speak about what I live.

TALK TO ME

I was walking through Utah when a woman stopped in a little blue Volkswagen. She and her two small children were crying. She said, "Would you talk with me? I need someone to talk to." It seemed she and her husband were having problems and they were thinking of breaking up.

I said, "Sure, I'll be glad to help." After we talked for awhile, she started feeling better. Then she asked if I would come home and talk to her husband. I said, "I'll try."

So I went to their house with her and we sat outside for about twenty minutes, talking. Her husband finally came out, looking angry. He said, "What's going on here?"

She said, "It's not what you think. This man is living what our parents have been preaching to us. I wanted him to come over. Maybe he can help us."

127

Her husband looked a little unsure at first. Then he said, "Well, come on in."

We sat down at the kitchen table, but he acted as if he wasn't listening to anything that was being said. Then, after about an hour, he just broke down and started crying. He put aside his fears and told his wife everything that was bothering him. After he let it all out, they hugged and kissed and made up.

I ended up staying for dinner and spent the night. The next day, they took me about 200 miles towards where I was going.

They said that, since they were going to stay together, they'd probably move to a little cottage in the area.

A year or so later, I was back in their area. It was a Sunday, so the post office was closed and I didn't know their address. I sent them the thought that I was here, but I didn't know where they lived, and could they come get me?

About ten minutes later, a car pulled up and out jumped the wife. She ran over and gave me a big hug. Her husband was right behind her, saying "I don't understand it. We were talking to our neighbor, and I suddenly decided to go visit my parents. But I've never driven this way to see them."

I said, "Well, I was calling you to come and get me."

"And here we are!" he laughed.

HIT MAN

One day, my daughter Kristina and I were hitchhiking to California. She was about fifteen. A man picked us up in Iowa and said he was going to Denver. When we got to Highway 84 going south in Nebraska, my inner voice said, "Get out and go south."

So I said to the driver, "Stop, we're going to get out here."

"No, Dad, we've got a ride all the way to Denver. Let's keep going," Kristina urged.

But I couldn't do that. "No, Kristina," I told her. "I've got to follow the guidance within me."

So we got out and began walking south on Highway 84 when a van with two men and a woman in it picked us up. We drove for several hours, and the whole time, Kristina and the other three people did all the talking. I sat in the back, silently chanting.

When they dropped us off and we were walking down the road, I said, "Kristina, those people were crooks."

"No, Dad. They couldn't be," she argued. "They were too nice."

I said, "Maybe they were nice, but they were crooks. There have been a lot of nice people over the years who were crooks."

So, about half an hour later, I saw their van coming back towards us again. When we got in, they told us they'd been worried about Kristina. They thought maybe I had kidnapped her.

I felt it was time to speak to them about what I did in life. After an hour or so, one of the men started crying. He told us that he had been a hit man. So we talked for the next couple of hours about forgiveness and about why we were here on this planet. When we got out of the van, the hit man was a different person. I felt he had been saved.

Kristina looked at me and said, "I've never seen anything like that, Dad. That was truly a miracle. Thank you."

PENSATIA

Ever since I had read the book that described "a red-haired man who would walk and wave," I had wanted to find Pensatia, the author. I found out that she lived in Miami, and when I finally made it down there, I was able to locate her. She was living in a run-down hotel in a seedy part of the city.

Once I found her room, I saw several locks on the door. I wondered why this woman who wrote so much about spirituality lived with so much fear. Usually, people who are aware have no need for locks.

I knocked on the door, and at first Pensatia wouldn't let me in. But when I told her who I was, she opened the door. We talked for about an hour.

But we didn't talk about me. Instead, for the full hour, we talked about relationships. The reason Pensatia was so afraid was that her boyfriend had left her six months earlier. At first, she had been depressed. Later, her depression had turned to fear.

By the time we had finished talking, Pensatia's fear was gone.

I had thought that, by going to see Pensatia, I would learn more about myself. But I think the real reason I was sent there was to thank her for her book by helping her heal her sadness.

By the way, at the time Pensatia was eighty-three years old. No matter how old we are, we can be healed when somebody gives us love.

12

Beauty in Strange Disguises

Love is the only true beauty.

PRETTY IS AS PRETTY DOES

One Memorial Day, I was hobbling with a shattered kneecap on my way to Utah. Everyone else was celebrating the holiday, but I was alone and in so much pain, I was almost in shock.

I knew I had to lie down, but all I had was $15. I began to look for a motel, and finally spotted one nearby. At that time, motels usually cost about $15. I walked over to this one, and was met by a sweet-looking woman at the desk.

(At the time, I thought I wasn't judging anymore —I'd "transcended" judging, you know).

I looked in this woman's eyes and they just seemed to glow and shine with spiritual awareness. So I thought, "Thank goodness. I've got it made. With her consciousness, she's going to let me stay."

I began, "I know your rooms probably cost more, but all I have is $15. Can I possibly get a room?"

"Oh, no," she answered." Our cheapest room is $20."

So I said, "Okay, thank you," and I went out and hobbled to the end of town. There was another motel, the last motel in town. And this was the last town in Utah for about a hundred miles.

I knew this was my last chance, and I was a little nervous. But I knocked on the door and walked in, and there was a woman who looked like a witch. In fact, she looked so crabby I immediately thought, "Oh, man, there's no way she's gonna let me in!"

But I decided to give it a try.

"I'm sorry," I began. "All I have is $15. But I was in an accident last night, and I'm really in a lot of pain. I need to lie down and soak in a tub," I told her. She could see I was in pain as I spoke to her.

"Well, honey, of course," she said. "You only have $15? Here, you keep $5 to eat with. You just pay $10."

What a beautiful lesson I learned that day about judging appearances!

BERTHA

Picture this woman. She's just zoomed by me in a wheelchair in the Park Lane Mall in Reno. She has no legs and only stumps for arms. But as soon as she went by me, I felt such a beautiful energy coming from her! After going a little way down the mall, she turned back towards me, and I saw that she was scarred more than anyone I have ever seen.

I thought, "Wow! I'd like to talk to her." Then, I heard ZZZZ as she pulled up in front of me in her motorized wheelchair. I just felt so thrilled.

We began to talk, and she told me that many years before, she had been a dancing teacher in Los Angeles. Then, her car had blown up, and she had lost her legs and most of her hands. Her whole body was now a scar, except for her beautiful eyes.

As she sat before me, I felt how powerful her energy was, and even though she was so scarred, I found her beautiful.

After we talked a bit, she asked me if I accepted donations. I said, "Sure." So she placed a bill in my hand. Later, after we had said goodbye, I looked down and saw that it was a hundred-dollar bill.

Thank you, Bertha, for the money and for your inner beauty. What an inspiration you are!

13

Unlikely Teachers

No one can judge another's path.

GOURMET GARBAGE

The year I went to Washington to tell President Ford about world peace, I slept behind the Lincoln Memorial in a sleeping bag. I was pretty much alone.

Then, the day before I left, I was sitting on the steps of the Memorial when an old man with the biggest backpack I ever saw walked by. As soon as I saw him, it came to me that he was to teach me something.

So I went over to him as he was washing his

feet in the Reflection Pond, and asked him how long he had been traveling. He didn't answer.

Three times I asked him, and three times he didn't answer. In those days, I didn't have the patience to let him be silent. So I said, "You know, I've been traveling for three years, and I wouldn't treat another person the way you're treating me."

When I said that, he looked up at me and smiled. He told me that he had been traveling since 1935. I said, "Well, I know how I've been surviving, but how have you been surviving?"

He answered, "I get my food out of garbage cans."

Then, he told me his story. It turned out he was the Howard Hughes of garbage can collectors. He would go around the country to memorial places and parks just to sample the garbage.

Finally, the old man asked me if I wanted to have lunch with him. I was curious as well as hungry, so I said, "Sure."

Well, he broke out the food, and boy, did we have a feast. He'd wait until the tour buses with the children had gone, and then he'd go searching for leftovers. He would never take anything that had been bitten into.

We talked for a couple of hours. Then, just before we parted, I told him, "You know, in all my travels, you are one of the most peaceful souls I have ever met."

After we said goodbye, I asked myself, "What did I learn from him?" The answer came right back to me: I realized that he had no ego when he went into the garbage cans.

I wondered what that felt like, so I went over to a garbage can and started searching through it. At first, I felt funny because people were looking at me. Here I was, a healthy man going through the garbage. My pride didn't want them to think I was a bum.

But I kept searching and then I found an open can of beans. I ate from the can of beans with my fingers. They tasted great! When I finished them, my ego had floated away, and I felt as if tons of weight had been lifted from me.

I've heard people say that the ego has to die for God to come forth. I don't feel that way.

The way I see it, the ego just opens up to the God within us all.

LOVE WITHOUT JUDGMENT

One day, I was down in the Bowery in New York City. A young man came up to me and asked me for some money. He was trying to get a bus ticket to go home to Minnesota. He was quite clean-cut and looked Scandinavian—he really did look as if he'd come from Minnesota.

I told him, "All I have is $5, but you can have it. It won't get you all the way to Minnesota, but it will help."

Three years later, I found myself back on the same street corner, and there the young man was, wearing the same clothes. But now he was filthy dirty and he looked thirty years older.

I went up to him and said, "Remember me, I gave you that $5 three years ago?"

He didn't seem to hear me and just babbled away. I walked off, but the next day I found him lying in the gutter just a couple of blocks away. This time, he looked up at me and cried out, "Oh, please help me, please help me."

I sat down on the curb and put his head in my lap. I started stroking his forehead and the top of his head. Then I began crying, asking God why we have to go through these painful experiences.

Suddenly, a voice said, "Let him be, it's his path to find Me." I knew that I couldn't change the path this man was on, so the best gift I could give him was to keep sending him love and understanding.

It wasn't easy for me to do it, but I got up and left him in the gutter. As I slowly walked away, I thought about how our paths take us to different places—and that just might include lying in a gutter some day. So when we come across someone who's there, all we can do is to keep loving them, no matter what.

And if it's their path, someday they'll get out of the gutter.

BAG LADY LOVE

New York is always such a wonderful place to visit because anything can happen there. I was visiting the city once, standing on the corner of 47th Street and the Avenue of the Americas. A little old lady about 4'9" tall came up to me and asked if I would buy her a sandwich. I said, "Yes, I'd be delighted."

I went into a nearby deli and bought her a great big bologna and cheese sandwich. When I gave it to her, she said, "Here, you eat some first." So I took a couple of bites and she ate the rest. She told me her name was Diane, and we talked for about an hour. Then, we said goodbye.

A day or two later, I was walking down 5th Avenue and I saw Diane coming towards me. She sort of fell into me and said, "Oh, you're that nice young man who bought me that sandwich the other day. I've been thinking a lot about you.

You're different than most of the people I meet. Would you come and talk with me?"

"Sure," I told her.

"But I have to lie down," she said. "I'm so tired, I'm about to fall over."

She told me about a place a few blocks ahead, where she often slept. So we walked until we found the stairwell, and went up to her special place. Then, she asked me to find her a piece of cardboard she could lie down on. I looked around and spotted a nice padded piece. She was so tickled, it was as if I had bought her a house.

Diane lay down for a rest, and I lay down beside her and began to chant. I chanted with her for about two hours.

At one point, I looked down, and here was this lady in her late 70's lying there asleep, stinking and dirty. My heart just opened up to her, and I felt the love just pour into me. I kept chanting and sending her love, and it felt as if she was teaching me an important lesson.

Then she woke up, and I asked her if she would like to come to Reno with me. She said,

"Yes, I would. Then I could see those beautiful paintings on the wall." To my surprise, she began to describe my friend Betty's living room. (I live with Betty sometimes when I'm in Reno). I have no idea how she knew about Betty's paintings, but she was able to see them in her mind's eye.

I told her I would meet her in a week or so, and we could hitchhike back to Reno. A week later, I found her rummaging in a garbage can. "Hi, Diane," I said. But she looked at me as if she'd never seen me before. Then I realized that Diane had gone back to the inner world she had lived in before I met her.

I guess that whole experience was about sharing those two loving hours on the stairwell.

PART 3

---

*Healing
the Spirit*

14

Losing Theresia

Sometimes we have to move from heartbreak
to love and understanding.

FAREWELL TO A DAUGHTER

When my daughter Theresia died at the age of thirty-four, I had the biggest heartbreak I've ever experienced.

Chad, her sixteen-year-old son, found her. He had been walking down the basement stairs looking for her and calling her name. Suddenly, he heard his mother say, "Chad, I'm not down there, I'm right here next to you."

My nephew was scared, but he went down into the basement. Then he saw his mother hanging there. Somehow, he was able to cut her down. Then he ran upstairs crying and screaming and trying to find the phone to call us.

Bonnie called Theresia's doctor a week later, and found out that cancer had spread all through her body. We were all in shock.

A month later we were having a garage sale, and someone found these letters in a box.

Mom,

Oh, my wonderful Mother! When God created you, he had Wonderful in mind. You're the warmest, kindest person God ever created.

You taught me so much about life, love, giving and sharing. You always made me feel safe and sure of myself, and that I could do anything.

If there was anyone in this world I could have been like, it would be you. Mother, you gave me so much more than you can ever imagine. You are the dearest to my heart.

I love you, my mother. We will truly and always be one!

I love you, Mom,

Theresia

Dad,

Hey, Moldy—couldn't go without saying that one last time. Dad, you're one of a kind! You taught me how to be forgiving and to have faith in the world around me.

Although at times we did not see eye-to-eye on some matters, I always respected your feelings and never tried to change you.

I love you, Father, and don't feel bad for not being around as much as you wished you could have. We all know that you were proud of us and loved us all as daughters.

See you in the comos, Daddy.

There were also letters to Cecelia, Sheley, and Kristina. Each letter was filled with love and appreciation for her sisters.

Finally, there was one last letter.

To All,

Well, by now Mom has read all the letters out loud and everyone knows how special each one of you were to me.

As a family I couldn't have asked for a more loving and open family. You all, in a special way, touched my life deeply. Please don't be sad.

Know that I lived a happy life. My only regret was that I didn't get to spend enough time with you all, but the time I did spend was priceless. Remember how much I love you all and how happy I was to be a part of your lives.

Be good to each other and live life to its fullest. I did.

Love, Theresia

Theresia, honey, you taught me more than anyone else that we each have our own path. But it hurt so much. Now the hurt has opened me up to even more love and understanding. Thank you, my darling daughter and friend.

15

Life Lessons

Patience, my dear ones . . .

"SLOW DOWN" #1

I was walking in Reno one day when I met a man who owned a used car lot in town. He gave me a lift and we began to open up to each other, talking and sharing. When he dropped me off, he asked, "What can you do to help me find peace?"

I said, "Well, I suggest you try to slow down a little bit and become more still within yourself. Take some time each day to be still."

I saw him a few years later. He told me he went home that night and put the written message I'd given him on the glass under the coffee table.

Some time later, he had a stroke. And when he got to the hospital, the doctors discovered that he had cancer, and amputated his leg.

"You told me to slow down, remember?" he told me. "Well, I think all of that happened to slow me down, because believe it or not, I'm happier now than I've ever been in my life!"

"SLOW DOWN" #2

Miss Donna, a friend of mine, was driving down the street really fast, and shouted, "Hey, Ed!" to me as she sped by.

"Slow down! Slow down!" I answered her. A couple of minutes later, she got up on the freeway and wrapped her car around a telephone pole.

Later, I talked to the policeman who pulled her out. He said it was a miracle that she had survived. Miss Donna was a big woman, and they had to take her out of a very tiny space. By some miracle, the metal had been bent all around her, like a protective shell.

Donna was lucky. She escaped with a smashed leg—and her life. And she slowed down.

"SLOW DOWN" #3

My younger sister and her husband had a timeshare place up at Lake Tahoe. They would exchange their place for one owned by one of her husband's business friends. So I sometimes spent time up there with them.

At the time, my sister was really speeding around. It was "Yak, yak, yak." She just didn't stop. I'd been visiting the family for two nights, and hadn't been able to get a word in edgewise.

I didn't want to say anything to her directly, so I silently asked her to "Slow down, honey. Slow down a little bit."

She did. Shortly afterward, while racing around, she fell and broke her arm. Sometimes it takes a lot to slow us down, but if we need to take a break, we'll get it—one way or another!

PEACE FORMULA

A lawyer friend came to visit me one Thanksgiving. We talked about all kinds of things. Then he said, "I suppose you can give me five easy steps to find peace of mind, huh, Ed?"

I said, "No, I can give you two."

"What? What are they?" he asked, surprised that I already had an answer.

I said, "First, you get control of your mind by thinking a single thought. For example, for the first two years of waving, I focused on the phrases, 'All love and understanding fills my heart. All love and understanding shines throughout the world.'

"Second, you blend each thought with your breath. You inhale with the first phrase and exhale with the second. When I was given a sound, like Ka-Re-Rom, I did the same thing.

"When you do this breathing, you're stilling your mind so you can listen to Spirit. The phrase, 'Be still and know that I am God' is probably the most powerful one I've ever heard.

"Then, you'll receive wisdom that comes from your heart. And oh, that's the power and that's the peace and that's the understanding we all seek."

16

Looking Down
the Road

*I love you all so much, and I'm
looking forward to our paths crossing.*

PROMOTION TIME

I was walking and waving down the big hill
in Sedona in late 1996 when the words suddenly
came to me: "You keep this up, and you'll get a
promotion." Well, I just chuckled to myself and
made a note to watch for something coming.

A few days later, I was doing my chanting
and at the end of voicing my chant, I heard
myself saying, "Samadhi, Samadhi, Samadhi."

And with this new word, my life has changed. I'd experienced so much bliss these past twenty-two years with my chanting that I didn't think any more was possible. But since "Samadhi" came, I really feel as if I've been given a promotion. Someone told me "Samadhi" means "supreme bliss."

What a gift this is to someone who used to sign A.C.H. after his name—for "A Carpenter's Helper."

Epilogue

TALKING WITH "THE WAVER"

A conversation between Ed Carlson and Claire Gerus

C: *Do you think people are different when they're traveling? And if so, how?*

E: I think so. When they're traveling, they're more able to live in the present. When they're at home, or going to work, they're always anticipating the next thing they have to do, and they're in a rush to do this, do that....But time is kind of suspended on the road, unless it's one of those occasions when a person has to be somewhere and they're aware of the time.

C: *Often, when something unpleasant happens, people ask, "Why me?" What do you tell them?*

E: Some of our biggest lessons come through heartbreak, but people often ask, "Why did God do this to me?"

The answer is, "God didn't do it. God is pure love. God is pure light. We're here in this human form to 'experience the experience.' So everything that might look negative is just a lesson to get us back to our Source. Things that our minds think are negative or terrible or painful are just part of the human experience. So we need to be thankful for them."

That's how I've transcended them—just by thankfulness.

C: *So many people are afraid of the future: of disease, unemployment, desertion .... Is there an antidote to fear?*

E: To accept it, to be thankful for it. We're used to giving thanks for things that make us feel good. We forget to be thankful for the things that *don't* make us feel good.

Our truth on this planet is simple, but the mind makes it difficult. It just boils down to love. And each experience is here to teach us that.

C: *What have you learned over the years about giving?*

E: People often tell me that they're walking a spiritual path and that they "give." But they also admit that they often feel drained.

I tell them that feeling drained means they're not giving unconditionally; they're expecting something in return. If you're truly giving, you can't be drained.

It's the same with my waving. If I got upset because someone didn't wave back, what a terrible job this would be!

So I just keep giving out, "I love you. I love you."

Loving has to be unconditional.

C: *What does your wave represent?*

E: To me, the wave represents "I love you." The one comment I keep getting from people over the years has been, "Ed, when I see you wave, it gives me hope."

In fact, I was told that a Catholic priest was giving a woman her last rites, and she had one final request: "Would you tell that man who waves how happy he made my life?"

When he told me that, I just started to cry.

C: *If you had to put a label on yourself, what would it be?*

E: I think I'm kind of a disciple. When people used to ask me what I was, I'd say, "Well, I'm a Waver." Then, a couple of years ago, I heard myself say, "I'm a Carpenter's Helper." And when I heard those words, I thought, "I am!" and goose pimples came up.

Since I've gotten my promotion to Samadhi, I no longer feel like I'm an assistant. I'm working directly with the Source, and I feel blessed to be able to devote my whole life to serving others.

C: *Can you tell us why you sometimes give small stones to people? Where do they come from?*

E: Maybe three times a year, I'll go to Lake Tahoe. When I'm there, I pick up two or three buckets of stones and give them out. I might give a stone for patience, or prosperity, or love. There's a special energy from Lake Tahoe.

Sometimes I'll give someone a stone to heal a headache. I'll say, "Put that stone to your forehead," and the headache will go away. It could be that the stone has a low vibration and counteracts the electrical energy that causes the headache.

C: *Do you consider yourself a healer? Is that one of your gifts to others?*

E: No one's ever come to me for healing. It's always been spontaneous. If you try to do it, there's anxiety and that can block the healing.

I don't really consider myself a healer. I'm a spiritual being just like everyone else. We can all heal, we can all fly or walk through walls. It's just a matter of our spirits and our bodies becoming one.

C: *How do you feel about mental illness?*

E: I feel strongly that everything we're experiencing is to help us become one with God. So mental illness is also a way of becoming one with God. Because it's so misunderstood, we put a negative connotation on it. But that mentally ill person is just becoming one with God in a different way. It's as valid an experience as what we call "sanity."

C: *With which religion do you feel most strongly connected?*

E: I feel a strong connection with the yogis. People often ask me, "What are you? Christian? Buddhist?" I think all the religions are connected. When I read, *Autobiography of a Yogi,* I felt closest to the yogis.

I believe I'm from the lineage of Yukteswar. Once, back home in Reno, I had the best meditation experience ever, and I realized I was part of that lineage, even though I'm from the Western world.

I've been connected with many religions over many lifetimes, as I believe we all have been. And my message today is for everyone, regardless of religion.

Over the years, different groups would ask me to come and tell them my stories. I've talked to Unity Church, Science of Mind, Methodists and Baptists, and civic groups and associations.

Once I spoke to a group of businessmen at the Reno Chamber of Commerce. I wore levis and a shirt and a sheepskin vest. By the end of the evening, they said, "Ed, we've had a lot of speakers over the years, but you're the best." That was because I touched their hearts.

C: *You're living a very courageous life, following your own guidance. Many people would love to do that, but they're afraid of the consequences.*

E: People often say, "Ed, I wish I could just go and experience what you're experiencing. You look so happy, while I've got to work to support my family."

But I tell them, "I have so much respect for you. What you're doing is beautiful. And my path is different. People like me have been given the time to help balance the planet. That way, we can help those who don't have the time to do it."

C: *So everyone is helping in their own way. . .*

E: Yes, even the person in the gutter. Because we're all energy, and the homeless and the derelict and the drunk are part of the energy. They're there to help other people "non-react"—to love them no matter what they're doing.

C: *How do you feel about the universe and abundance? Do you believe it's always open to you, like a bank?*

E: Yes, the universe is always open to you, as long as you're open to the universe. I often say, "I open myself up to all that is." It feels so good to say that.

C: *How can we learn to live in the moment when we're so focused on the past and the future?*

E: Here's an example. Last Sunday, there was a girl at the Unity Church. She was an agent, but she wanted to become an actor. She said to me, "I've got to make a decision about what to do."

And I told her, "All you've got to do is be happy. When you are truly happy, the decision will be made for you."

C: *Why do you chant? Can others do it the way you do?*

E: I began chanting three years after I began walking. It's such a wonderful way to still my mind and let me listen to my heart.

Many groups give people a sound and tell them to keep it secret, not to share it with anybody. I have no secrets. My sound is your sound. It's universal. I want to share it with the world.

There have been different times over the last 22 years when, by chanting, I've reached plateaus where I felt, "How can it get any better than this?" Then my human side says, "Well, you can stop chanting now." But my Higher Self says, "You just keep doing what got you here. Don't stop, man."

Drawing of Ed by his friend Jessica, age 10.

Reflections on a Free Spirit

by Bonnie Carlson Mumm

FREE (His love is given readily and in profusion, unconditionally).

SPIRIT (God's divine influence working in the heart of man).

FREE SPIRIT—Ed has always been that, but back when we were younger, it was interpreted as a rebellious or troublesome quality because he wasn't "conforming"—even his mother didn't understand his behavior. She was probably his biggest critic, but she also would defend him to anyone who questioned her "Red."

My beliefs regarding any individual, Ed included, were—and still are—that we must allow each other to be. When it comes to other people, we have no control—their paths are already a given. Sometimes letting go is all that is needed to step to another level/plateau of existence for both the releaser and the "releasee." Let them go and they *will* come back!

Ed and I have had many experiences together, many good and some not so good. But Ed has always had a charismatic aura that makes people want to be in his presence (except for those few whose jaws felt the power of his fist!—you can't beat it into them, Ed). People want to hear his stories, and even many of those with whom he had confrontations found it easy to forgive and enjoy him. I believe I'm the best example—we are truly friends in the greatest sense of the word.

People *want* to know love—how to feel it, give it and receive it, how to *forgive* and be *forgiven*. These are some of the lessons Ed puts forth. His waving and smiling as he sends love up and down the highways and streets he walks, is sometimes met with scorn, gestures, harsh looks, and even—on a few occasions—the threat of physical harm.

But Ed continues to send his love, knowing it's what people really want; he continues to focus on his purpose and the overwhelming belief in the God in you, that the power of love will make you shine and that you, too, are a **FREE SPIRIT.**

**If you loved this book,
now you can listen
to Ed's stories
on audio tape.**

"I Walked to the Moon
and Almost
Everybody Waved"
by
Ed Carlson

60 minute audio tape
$12.95

To order, call
Stillpoint Publishing
at
1-800-847-4014
(Continental USA only)
or
603-756-9281

On the road with The Waver.

Farewell to Ed from friends in Sedona, AZ.